Of Rain

Tre'lon Grant

opening this book is an invitation into my mind;

tread with care.

they saw the sun in him, but never the rain that preceded it.

Rhythmic tapping of drops hitting the windshield
'04' mustang sheering diesel in a puff
sickness runs amuck
moods shift like the gauging of a clutch
call it a 'messy day' if you will
For most this is the nadir
the gunpowder gray sky
requiems presented by the raindrops
brisk zephyrs
two-toned roads
but for writers
this is the zenith
the days of clarity
these are days of wonderment
appreciation for the small things in life
the things that have long been forgotten
masqueraded by social media
cellular devices
blue light emitting machines
human escapade once was
the love of the unknown the
beauty of figuring things out for
oneself
I ponder what happened to us?

listen to the subtle droplets of rain
Pitter-patter on the window seal,
flickering burns keenly
tranquil toons echo.

singing prayers of health and light
over these times of twilight
erasing my soul's sore wounds away
the Art of War by Sun Tzu in my lap.

loving my neighbors as best I can
God's always right.
these times prove that nothing on Earth is
forever

no need for tears to be shed
recollect in the sun of the spirit, share that warmth
there's a cold around the corner
lift the spirit of the dampened; you can feel.

Darkened clouds
distant sun
Incoming night
hard rain
gusts of wind
deep breaths
walking right on through
It is nice to have friends
at times likes this

As rain clouds form
blued winds gust
leaves scatter
Escapade of norm
Behind the clouds
storms kick up dust
Crow hides under trees
man sheds a tear
.

if only i could
open locks for
A person that was
Once a locksmith
But with a broken
skeleton key the
Unsaids remain words
Written on a page
And a partition.

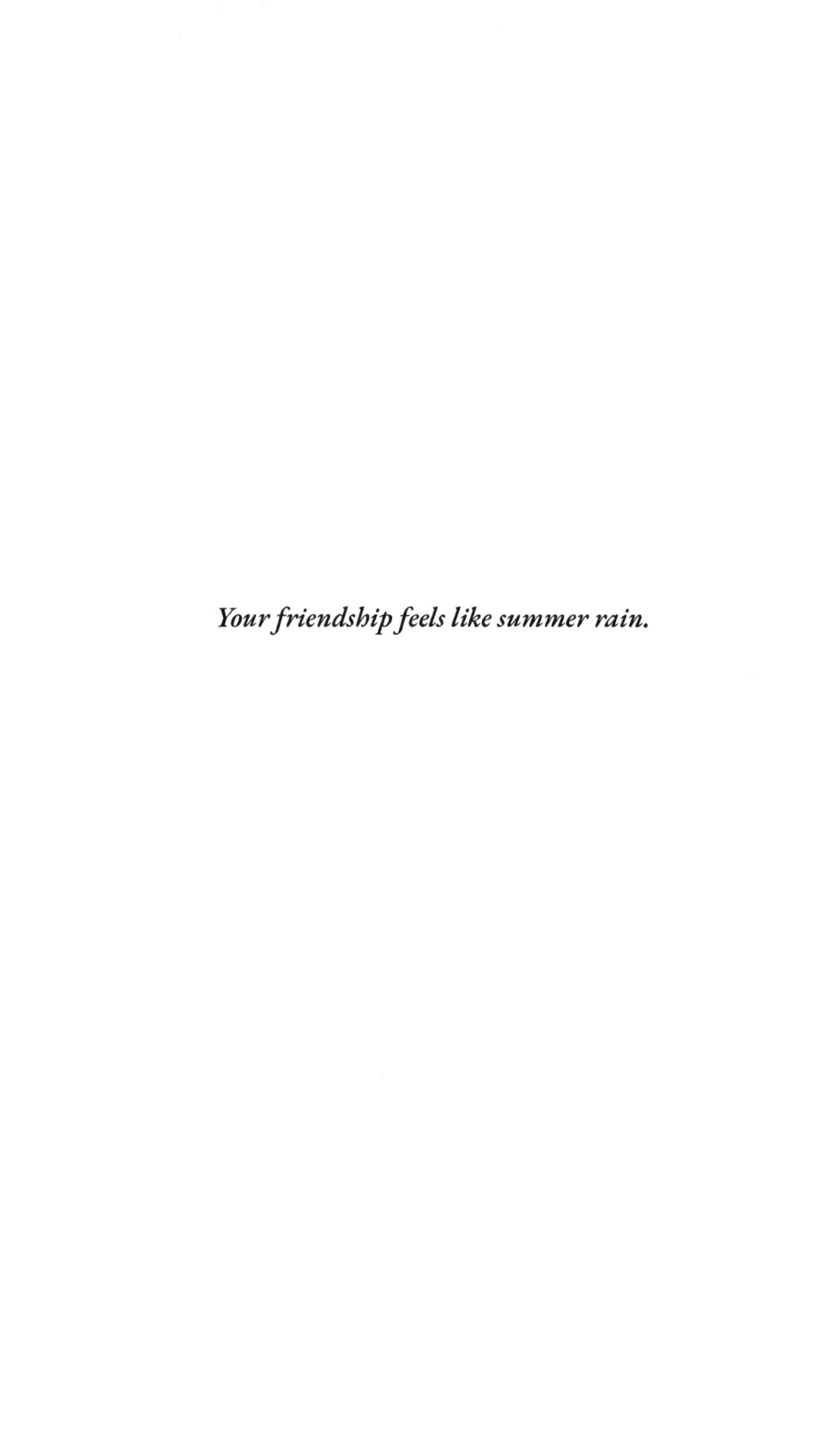

Your friendship feels like summer rain.

sylvan canopis overhang
Black birds perch
The subtle ant searches for food

.

.

.

how can i balance
A million things at once
The way a rainforest does?

.

.

.

Is it selfish of me to
wish for action more
Than words?

.

.

.

Evil of me to
Long for one to let me be still
Rather than the opposite

.

.

.

The toils of being human; the toils of having a
heart.

An eclipse, and a snow-filled field
The dusk is young, and rain drops flow.
Heart reverberates, intentions smoothed.
Frost on one's breath, and then gracious movement.

how can I make myself smile

And another?

Despite so much rain

A question to ask oneself every day.

we never truly know what we have, until it's gone.
An appreciation for people comes from
learning that all people deserve fairness,
love, reciprocation.

the trees will wither and die without the rain.
without the trees, the soil will become dust
the air toxic, and the rain will dissipate.
and without these, we cannot exist for mutualism -
cycle.

I've lost two from feelings of abjection.
their minds polluted by sadness, love absent.
they took their lives out of emptiness
a wrong focus.

Lessons we all must learn, and the lesson of loss is
an adversity
far too familiar to me; treat all with love
like I am called to do
Albeit it seems I still must learn to let go of what is
toxic...

But to keep loving, I'll never retract.

The mystery which never existed
but repeated
As they all talked about.

It never occurred
the scenes planted in their minds
never played out.

No one questions
none give answers
They leave it that way

They still fear
stay clear
Paranoid of the stillness

They shiver
when they hear
the dogs barking

they see shadows
in the lanterns, absence
but never forget their flashlights

they are all bound
everyone regrets

still stay at the edge

this chagrined community
awaits the rain
to wash away their stains.

azure akin gold
bronze akin scarlet
crimson darkens
until it becomes black.

aspects of light
one by one
occupy the
view.

low glow east
Full moon rises
Carelessly grinning at
me.

I grin back, and await the petrichor.

As I lie here in adoration, gaze fixed
toward the skies.
The stars, celestials brimmed with diamonds
luminous, radiant.
Their own archaic symphony, one wish we may all
choose
The moon of unequivocal beauty, a pillar for my
soul.
This gazebo I do lie below, sweet music
Drifts from birds above
A scent from rosebuds, an affirmation of true
natures love
A pond reflects alabaster skies, a dove
with cygnets laces the floor
The reflective pools of glorious lakes
under a scarlet orange sky, alone
with a notebook in one hand and
A pen in another
Away from the torturous nonsense
that has come my way
ruined my days
rained upon my soul.

Listen ....

they were broken before you.

stop trying to fix things you didn't break.

stop trying to fix people you didn't break.

Listen ... listen ....

It is not your responsibility to break yourself for somebody who is not ready to work on themselves.

It is not your responsibility to be the halcyon to a storm.

Stop it.

Let it go.

Why do we choose to focus the most amount of time on those that hurt us, forsaking those who choose to only love us? Human nature ... choosing the opposite of light, taking the hard road, no matter how many signs there are. Learning lessons, albeit.

Azure pools reflect
a nimbus sky
thunder cracks
reality pauses
time stands still
and motionless
we swim

have you ever felt the ruination of
something sacred coming?
Akin a coming storm, uprooting the ancient
trees and verdant grasses.
have you ever felt an uncanny, frightening
Feeling?
Like you know that something unpleasant is
coming?

.

.

.

have you ever watched as someone you
love forces distance, and no matter what
you do, the distance doesn't close?
have you ever had to prepare for the worst,
because as blindness, deafness, and muteness
asphyxiates
the ability to diagnose the true nature of the issue
one loses sight on how one is making others feel?

.

.

.

Well, it surely isn't a pleasant feeling.

hands outstretched
tears envelop my cheeks
heavy sighs
knees hit the ground
at the mercy of the storm above
such is the moment
one realizes they were wrong

the clouded sky paints the horizon a stormy gray.

one clear moment, one of trance
One missed step, one perfect dance
One missed shot, one and only chance
Life is all ... but one fleeting glance

To be like ... the Mulberry Tree.

in its annual glory
that outlasts the winter and
Stands strong in the storm
that may bend in the wind
But never break
rather grows ever so stronger

this is the definition of true friendship

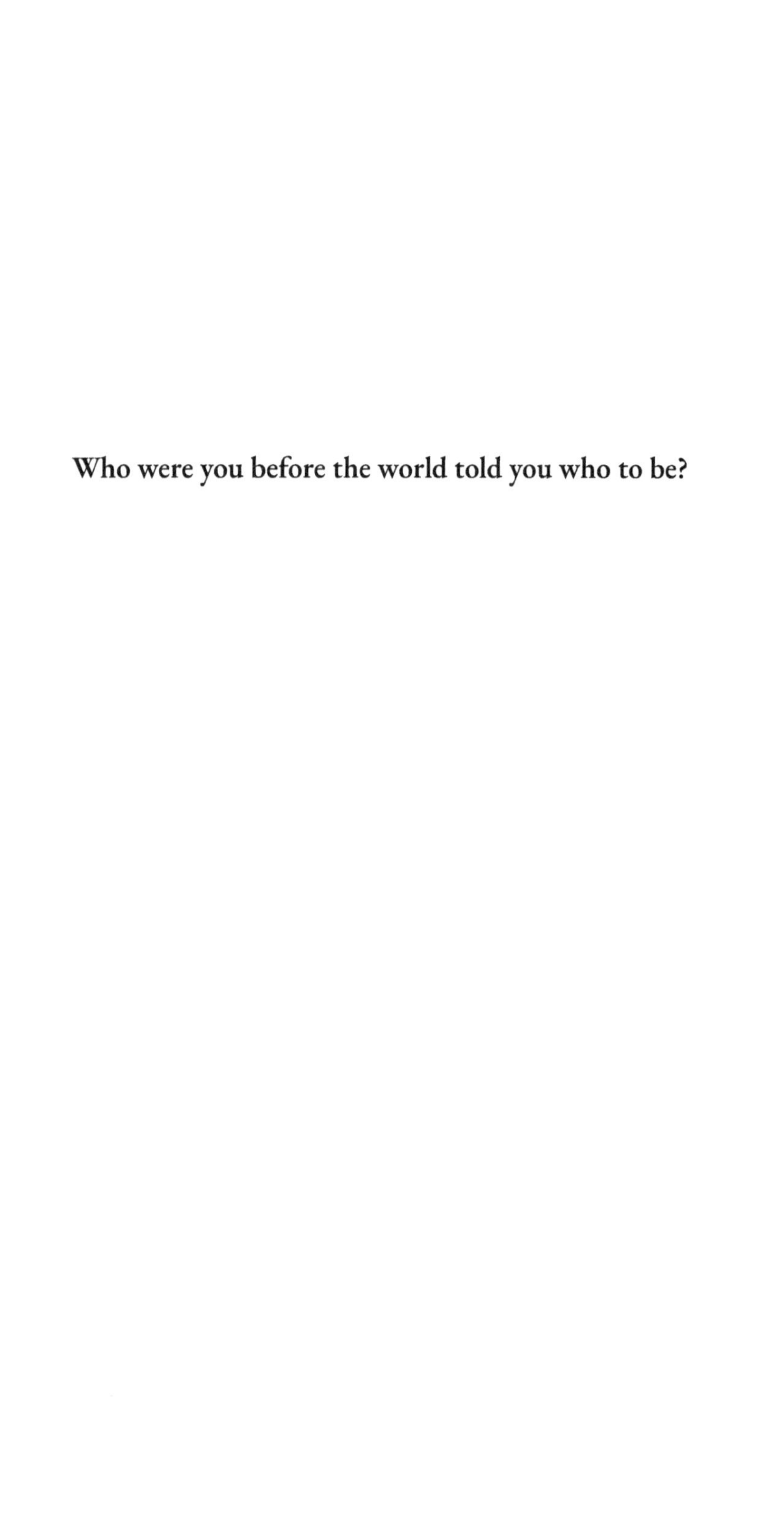

Who were you before the world told you who to be?

widespread rain descends
in the corner of my dreams;
A monsoon of drenching relief;
a tide to wash the slate clean.

I am a Man now;
Not a Boy.
And all of the wounds I've won
Unfurl across my body
And my soul
Like polished medals of valor
              Or one fragile, papyrus
            And thus garbed, and so adorned
            I will wade through the cooling
waters of
This cleansing storm.
Widespread rain descends
filling my outstretched arms;
Quenching the memory of the battle;
Bringing the strength to end the war.
I am worthy now.
I am enough.
And in my hand, I crush the dust
Of guilt, of shame,
Releasing these bitter grains

To the absolution that comes with
The drumming of
The rain.

the crack of thunder adjudicates the deep
Recesses of my mind, pulls my eyes back to
Bleaker skies where mistakes were made,
and the days were gray.
Those times, love was received, but rarely given,
realizations encased in brick
and eyes sealed shut.
A build-up that acted as a maelstrom, winds
heavy enough to blow everything around me away
as I sat in the eye of the storm safe and content.
Once it passed, I stepped outside to see nothing but
wreckage in wait.
I was the storm.

but even nightmares have endings, and storms come
to pass.
We wake up to a glorious morning sun or a
beautiful, radiant moon with different
opportunities knocking at our doors. More people
to love, to forgive, to reconnect with,
To lose someone that cared for you more than you
could imagine is a burning pain,
but to do so and not make any attempt to try is a
severance.
Our time is limited, yet love lasts forever.
Do right by all, fix things and restart.
Shed love everywhere and always.
That's all that matters.

You've made yourself too available
generous, free, easy
and sadly

people tend to underestimate the value
of things they get
for free.

It is said that love breaks the heart again and again
... until it stays open.

a stark reminder

entitlement, no

no one is entitled to anything.
Abandon that mentality.
No one is obligated to love you,

Instead, love *you*.

Do you love *you*?

to harbor the pitfalls that befell my
yesterday only to ruin my tomorrow would
make me a fool in the present

*   *   *   and you

are * *

          *   just like the storms
*   *

*   * * so fervent

* * you dance beautifully * *
* * * illuminating the night sky * * *
* * *   at the darkest * * *
* * *   of   * * *
times * * * *
*   *   *   *   *

It's often that our deepest hatreds tend to be the
very things we cannot change about ourselves.

never ignore the inexplicable
there are many lessons
hidden in bewilderment

going home doesn't always entail
returning to a place
sometimes
it's simply returning to yourself

When the periphery is muted
one walks the precipice
long and narrow

Open minds are fenced in;
And are inadvertently confined
to hushed tones
and feeble babbles.

Life then ceases to be a journey...

But rather,

a recurring commute.

Actions
Outweigh
The Cacophony of sugared words

Or
When coupled together, two planets join
The best of both worlds

A rarity, a fresh rain

Be that somebody.

oh how i've missed me
and when the sun and moon align
i'll beckon the stars closer
than they have ever been before
whenever that might be

the way you love
says a lot about you.

but the way you break
says a lot about where you came from.

a looming rainstorm.

scattered raindrops
hectic wind chimes
suffocating pressures
out of sync with life

if only we pondered about how others might feel

Before securing so much

Comfort in what makes us happy

.

.

for in the end, what we do for others is what

matters most.

y la lluvia ....

finalmente pasa.